Healing Our Animal Friends With EFT

by
Andrea Christos

authorHOUSE®

AuthorHouse™
1663 Liberty Drive, Suite 200
Bloomington, IN 47403
www.authorhouse.com
Phone: 1-800-839-8640

First published by AuthorHouse 2/18/2009

ISBN: 978-1-4389-1470-1 (sc)

Printed in the United States of America
Bloomington, Indiana

This book is printed on acid-free paper.

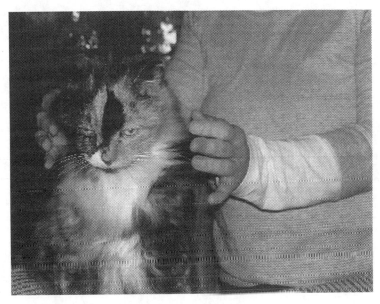

Luna, my inspiration

Thanks to Mike, Sahfi and Liela
who make all things possible

TABLE OF CONTENTS

To The Reader ix

Introduction xi

Chapter One: Memories 1

Chapter Two: How Does EFT Help Animals? 17

Chapter Three: What Are We Tapping For? 21

Chapter Four: Formula For Tapping... 25

Chapter Five: Some D.I.D Tapping Possibilities.................................... 35

Chapter Six: When Does EFT For Animals Not Work?....................... 41

Chapter Seven: Addressing Imbalanced Behavioral Problems 47

Chapter Eight: Inspiration 53

Author 59

Proceeds... 61

Memorandum... 63

To The Reader:

This workbook has been designed keeping in mind that the information and the concept being conveyed is probably unfamiliar and new to you.

I could have filled hundreds of pages with thousands of words, but in my opinion, this was unnecessary and would have obscured the simple format and technique being put forth. One of the benefits of this practice is that it is simple. It is the simplicity of this technique that yields such an easy and meaningful reward for us and for the animal being treated.

The pages are letter sized so that the "tapper" can leave the book open in order to refer to the tapping options suggested while simultaneously stroking the pet being helped. These larger pages and type make it easier to read. It also leaves room for making notations as you progress.

Please keep in mind that Healing Our Animal Friends With

EFT is

    simple;

    direct;

    uncomplicated;

    easy to use and

    fun to share.

Please enjoy this workbook which is intended to be a simple gift for you, just as Healing Our Animal Friends With EFT is meant to be a simple but powerful gift for your animals.

Andrea Christos

INTRODUCTION

EFT stands for Emotional Freedom Technique. This technique, founded by Gary Craig, is being used worldwide to help countless numbers of people and animals regain good health and personal well-being. Please refer to the EFT web site www.emofree.com for a detailed and thorough understanding of this process. At www.emofree.com you will also be able to locate EFT practitioners in your area who can give you personal assistance or guidance if you so desire.

HELPING OUR ANIMAL FRIENDS WITH EFT is a simple and effective method for creating positive change in the lives of our animal friends. Emotional and physical well-being can be obtained by simply tapping gently up and down their spines several times. This seems unlikely, I know, but until you have tried this, it is impossible to comprehend the simple effectiveness of this process. I have been using this with great success for some time. It is my belief that anything that lives upon the Earth has basically the same needs, desires and concerns. Humans, horses, cattle, dogs, cats, birds and lizards all basically want to survive happily, safely and comfortably.

Domesticated animals, I believe, have the most difficult time of it because they cannot fend for themselves. They are living in a very unnatural state, having surrendered their independent capability for survival over to mankind. Evidence tells us that mankind cannot always manage their own affairs in a compassionate, abundant and ethical manner. Often the animals suffer terribly because they fall prey to human violence, ignorance and neglect. The purpose of this book is to provide relief for our animal friends who are in need and to offer a simple guide for those who wish to help.

Please use this manual to help your pets, your friends and your friends' animals. It is my highest wish that this simple but effective method will be implemented as a beneficial practice for veterinarians, S.P.C.A. workers, animal welfare professionals of every kind, and for each household in which a pet resides.

Use EFT For Animals wherever you think there is a need. Use it when the animal is struggling physically and/or emotionally. This is, of course, not expected to replace veterinary care if the animal is sick or injured. However, it will help prepare a sick or injured animal to receive care by being more receptive and less fearful, and it will help the animal to recover more swiftly and completely.

Once you have practiced this, you will be amazed at the simplicity of the technique and the success you will have. Teach your children to do EFT for their pets as well. Often children are very successful because they have an easy way of knowing what an ailing or fearful pet may be experiencing. Often young people tend to be less burdened by a tendency to over-think things, and that is helpful. Not complicating this technique is a definite plus. Of course children should never be expected to be around animals who pose even the slightest danger to them.

On the emofree web site you will see that the tapping points, originally designed for humans, are generally on the front of the body and hands. This procedure allows us to help others but also enables us to treat ourselves as well. For our purposes in working with animals it is unrealistic to tap on their faces and or feet. Often the animals we are working with are excited and agitated, making it dangerous for the tapper and too threatening or disquieting for the animal to accept. Most animals would not be comfortable being tapped, even lightly, around the face and feet, paws or claws especially when they are under stress.

Throughout my life I have been doing healing work mostly with/for humans. The basis of my work has been addressing the emotional and physical imbalances within us with intuitive insight and bio-energetic touch. Throughout my professional life, all forty years of it, I have studied and continue to study anything in my field that furthers and enhances the effectiveness of my work.

It is exciting to me that after all these years new developments and options are being made available. These are options that provide us with a healing tool that anyone can use for themselves, their friends/family and for their animals as well.

EFT is a tool that anyone, anywhere can use to make real and vital change in their health and well being.

WHY EFT??

- Results are practically instant.

- Painless.

- Not traumatizing.

- Easy to understand.

- Gentle.

- Doesn't require tools or materials.

- Doesn't require a detailed knowledge of animal anatomy.

I have found that tapping up the spine and across the head of the animal works just fine. Most living beings have a spine which is relatively close to the surface, easy to locate, and simple to access.

Therefore, all of the work we will be presenting in this book will be done by simple, gentle tapping along the length of the spine.

Try doing EFT with your animals when they are most relaxed, comfortable and receptive. This workbook has been designed to be easily understood so that you can refer to it while tapping on your animal friends. Keep in mind that this technique is simple; direct and uncomplicated. Refer often to this manual, to our web site and to the EFT web site. Share your successes with friends and family, and stay open to suggestions from them.

I wish you every success in your endeavor to help our animal friends.

All The Best,

Andrea V. Christos

CHAPTER ONE
MEMORIES

If you did not care for and respect animals, you probably would not be reading this. Concern and respect for animals is the very reason I have written this workbook, hoping to share with others, a simple technique for the physical and emotional healing of our animal friends. Like many of you, my fondest memories are of those animals that I have loved and cared for and who have loved and cared for me. Many times I have shared with friends that "If it has four feet and fur, I love it." Just the sight of horses or deer grazing in a field or pasture makes the day a little brighter. Watching a flock of geese flying in a V southward or returning home, means that the seasons are changing, and reminds me that I am a part of the pageantry of planet Earth and her inhabitants. Seeing the parade of city dogs coiffed and shampooed makes me smile. Although she requires no coiffing or fluffing of any kind, Ruby is a perfect example of this. She is a Boston Terrier puppy and when Ruby comes to work with her person Sally, my day is made complete.

Ruby's arrival is the highlight of my day. Especially when I look out of the window, on the 29th floor, and see Ruby chasing a ball on the walled-in roof of the floor below. Another devoted animal lover, Rose, works at the desk on the first floor. When I come in to work Rose will tell me whether or not the goddess Ruby has arrived. She will report whether or not Ruby is wearing her rain jacket that day, or if she seems to have grown significantly over the holidays. There are thirty floors in this building, and probably a thousand people, but Rose and I only have eyes for Ruby.

In the not so distant past, I remember my own words declaring that I would happily trade all the men in my life (my father being the exception) for one good dog. While relaxing on my back porch a few years ago I watched my West Highland Terrier play in the garden. It was then that I realized that I actually had done exactly that. There was just Wilbur, the wonder dog, and me. And there was contentment.

Wilbur

Wilbur and I made a good team. We climbed mountains together, played in mountain streams and rested on mountain ledges and peaks, while watching clouds and some leaves drift by. Not all memories with Wilbur were blissful or content.

Memories are memories, some are good and some are not so good, but memorable just the same.

Every morning Wilbur and I would take our walk on a path that bordered a meandering stream. Willy was an incorrigible terrier who loved, above all else, a good fight. If he heard a dog fight taking place in the distance, he couldn't get there fast enough to enter into the skirmish. More than once did I have to risk life and limb to extract the little bugger from deadly combat. Of course the girls love a bad boy and Wilbur had many female admirers.

One of Wilbur's admirers was a white and pink bull terrier named Arabella. Arabella had it in her head that Wilbur was Mr. Studly and would always try to come between Wilbur and myself. One day we were taking our morning walk when Arabella and her person arrived on the scene. We could let our dogs run freely off-leash because we lived in an area with a very small human population. The dog population was probably equal to human.

On this particular day in early Spring the earth was wet and sloppy with ice and ice water. The wind was bitter and I wasn't in the mood to deal with Arabella's romantic demands upon Wilbur, who could not care less. I shooed her away with my foot. Arabella came up from behind and head-butted me with her huge, bony terrier skull. My feet went out from under me and I fell into the ice water and mud. Before I could stand up to challenge the thwarted suitor of my canine Lothario, Arabella came up from behind and head-butted me again. Finally, her person caught up to Arabella and leashed her, saving her from my wet and frigid wrath.

Dogs like Willy have a lot of character and leave a lot of memories.

One day Wilbur and I were walking to the post office. One had to time visits to the post office judiciously, because in a small town there were certain hours when it seemed like every village resident was there picking up their mail. If you weren't interested in spending hours catching up on the local gossip and community news, then it would be best to time your visits accordingly.

As Wilbur and I strolled through the post office parking lot we noticed a woman standing by her car motioning for us to come over to her. It turned out that she was a German woman who had a fourteen year old West Highland Terror, sorry, Terrier in her car. She explained to us that her dog had not, in fourteen years, given her a kiss. She wondered if Wilbur would be so kind as to do the honors. As we learned earlier, Willy is a dog with an overabundance of passion and lust of all kinds, so he was all too willing to slather a total stranger with a thousand wet and smelly dog kisses. She was happy.

The interesting thing about this experience was not the kiss, but she explained that her Westie, who watched quietly through the car window, was only calm and quiet when the dog outside of the car was a West Highland like himself. If any other dog came near his home or his car the dog would go ballistic with indignation and aggression.

I thought a lot about this on the walk home. There was a lot to learn from this experience. Because the Westie in the car was raised and loved by his mother and his pack, he knew that they were the providers of the safety, protection and nurturing that he needed to survive and grow as a puppy. It made me think about how difficult it must be for domestic animals to be culled from the safety and familiarity of their pack, pride, herd or flock. They are abruptly separated at infancy from the safety of their own kind and taken into homes, stalls, cages or kennels and tended to by a species completely unfamiliar to themselves. How terrifying.

Later in this book we will revisit this situation. As animal healers and helpers we must always remember to help them with the fundamental aspect of abandonment and loss that will stay with them throughout their lives.

Dogs, of course, haven't cornered the market on "cute". They probably think they have, but we know that it's not so.

The Coo-Coo's Nest

One of my favorite animals is my cousin's cat, Bella. Bella is an engaging little grey tiger cat with a big nose. Not a big, bulbous nose, but the aquiline Roman nose like that of the Egyptian Mau. She is lovely and lively and has a queer little habit that I would like to share with you.

Cousin travels quite a bit and was showing a prospective cat-care person through her house. They visited the kitchen, dining room and living room, while Cousin introduced the care person to the cats as they appeared during the tour.

When they opened the bathroom door they stopped abruptly, shocked to see Bella sitting inside the toilet bowl, gazing at them over the open seat. Cousin, blase' but amused, had seen this many times before, but the interviewee was stunned. The common belief is that cats loathe water, so we have little frame of reference for seeing a happy cat splashing and frolicking in a toilet bowl.

Bella In The Bowl

Cousin lives in her little "coo-coo's nest" with four distinct, but very different cats. They are all shelter or rescued cats who have found a safe and happy home with her. The group consists of Princess, Smokey, Ralphie and little Bella, the water nymph.

Cousin rescued Princess and her litter mates from the streets of Denver. She is probably thirteen years old now and the Dowager Princess indeed! She still maintains some feral tendencies and prefers to spend her days outside beneath the porch. If she is required to remain inside, she remains comfortably aloof and irritated. If all this imposed domesticity gets on her fragile nerves she isolates little Bella to spend her wrath upon.

Smokey is a 20+ lb., grey Maine Coon cat. He is an angel and the peacemaker. Mostly he lounges and blesses others with his soulful gaze. When Princess has decided to harass Bella, Smokey quietly steps in between them to put an end to the aggression. Afterwards he returns to his favorite place for napping and dreaming beautiful angel dreams.

And then there is Ralphie, the rascal! Cousin has always had an eye for the tuxedo cat colors. The sharp contrast between black and white caught her eye one day as she dared to walk past the area in Pet Smart where they display cats who are in need of homes. Lucky for Ralphie that Cousin was open to impulse buying that day. She saw him lying there terribly alone, seemingly sad and depressed. The deal was sealed. Cash was exchanged, the papers were signed and Ralphie was on his way to live with Cousin at the "coo-coo's nest".

Realizing his good fortune Ralphie was liberated from his malaise at once. He was immediately at home. Being an energetic juvenile he hit the ground running. He is turning into quite a large cat but still flies through the air with the greatest of ease. He loves to swing from the draperies; thinks nothing of breaking Cousin's favorite lamp, and when he is bored, torments little Bella. Although he and cousin have had many encounters with the squirt gun and the lectures, Ralphie could care less. He is free and happy.

The Business of Birds

We are grateful for the gift of wild birds in our lives. They awaken us at dawn with their early-bird chirping, morning crowing and melodic song to harken the arrival of the morning sun. Certainly a much kinder and more welcome way to great the day than the horrible screaming of the alarm clock. Whether they are living in the wild or domesticated; it matters not, for they are beautiful and intriguing to watch and joyful to hear.

When I was a child I loved visiting an older lady, Ms. Davenport, who lived nearby. She had a wonderful green Parakeet named Perky. Perky was free to fly around the house. He would sit on your shoulder and finger but I mostly enjoyed watching him take his morning bath. Ms. Davenport would put a few celery leaves in a bowl in the sink and let the cool water drip slowly onto the leaves. Perky loved his bath.

He would splash in the water, nibble on a few of the leaves and talk. He was a talker and had a lot to say.

When my children were young, we kept an assortment of chickens, not for their meat, but for their beauty and for the delightful interaction we enjoyed with them.

Somewhere, I have a photo of my eldest daughter swinging on her rope swing, which hung from an ancient black walnut tree outside of the kitchen door, her long hair flying, dappled by the summer sun. In her lap was a very large Rhode Island Red hen. The hen was laying on her back, feet upward, and was wearing the heart- shaped yellow sun glasses that my daughter had shared with her.

This particular daughter (we will call her Queenie) was devoted more to the birds than to the other animal members of our family. This is why it was her responsibility to play avian round-up at the end of each day to protect the chickens from hungry fox, owl, opossum and other nocturnal predators.

During the day, one could enjoy the sight of a Bantam hen named 'Honk', carrying her chicks nestled safely in her feathers. Tiny peeping heads peered out, while Honk instructed them in the art of daily life on the farm.

There was a fair amount of consternation as well when the aforementioned peeps, following their mother's instructions to eat the bugs that feasted on the blueberries and squash plants, ate the berries instead. For many summers we ate strawberries and blueberries that were higher than the head of a chicken or we suffered the indignity of eating leftovers with sizeable bird beak bites taken out of them.

On the farm, the evening sunsets created a special kind of peace and serenity. That comforting stillness would be severed abruptly by the whooping and hollering of Queenie, engaged in her task of herding errant chickens back into the coop.

For those who have not had experience with the nightly round-up of hysterical flocks of fowl, this requires a particular skill- set that Queenie was fortunately born with. Once the egg-layers were safely settled into their coop, she was off to shake the Bantam variety out of the trees. They, unfortunately, preferred to rest outside for the night. But the ever stalwart Queenie, was devoted to protecting them from nightly excursions of hungry land animals; opossum, fox, coyotes, racoon and just about any other animal that had a taste for plump yummy chicken.

Bantams maintain wild tendencies and don't think about flying predators such as owls, so Queenie would shake the trees, catching noisy flapping chickens as they plummeted toward the ground. Sometimes Queenie would catch one of the low -flying escapees with her bare hands, after which they were briskly, safely locked away in their little house, where they settled into a sound sleep. Perhaps dreaming of tomorrow's blueberry feast.

A special child in many ways, Queenie was seen catching a wild bird in flight as it made its way across our porch. I remember watching her in the creek catching fish with her bare hands. There, with hands swinging just above the water, swiftly and as accurately as a bear cub, she would catch the fish, usually a trout. Showing her friends the trophy and tickling it just for fun, she would drop it back into the flowing stream, resuming hunt pose ready for the next capture.

Sadly, and with regret, the time came when we had to leave the farm, our mountain-top refuge, for the flat lands with their mega-populations, poor eating habits, and destructive hyper-stimulation. We were in shock for awhile but eventually adapted to the madness of it all, although for me, without much enthusiasm or sincerity.

My youngest daughter whom I will refer to as Sweet Pea, was only 2 years old at the time and would miss out on much of the beauty and freedom we enjoyed as a family in our former rural life. She hasn't, however, missed out on the love and devotion we have for our animal friends. We have always had a house filled with neighborhood children and school friends, as well as a suburban assortment of domesticated furry, feathery and scaly members of our own family. Sweet Pea and her husband, even now while living in one of America's busiest cities, shares life with her two cats and cockatiels.

She taps herself daily to help avoid taking her allergy shots monthly, and her asthma medications daily, but nothing will prohibit her from sharing life with the animals to which she is completely devoted. She is also devoted to her husband. (Just thought I should mention this.) Together they ponder which dog would make the most suitable new addition to the group.

TIES THAT BIND

Comfort:

It has long been established that the act of touching or merely watching animals can have a measurable positive effect on the health of humans. It is gratifying that we can now return the favor with EFT For Animals.

Our animal friends bring to us a wonderful comfort that nothing else can convey.

What can be more relaxing and soothing than a cat's purr, or the soft snoring of a dog sleeping beside us on the couch or the floor below?

I find deep relaxation when I pause daily to brush my cat. There is a comforting completion when she sleeps on my legs or in my lap while I read.

Walking in the woods or in the neighborhood is always more relaxing when our dog walks beside us. If your dog does not walk beside you, but rather drags you down the street or runs off in the woods, it's time to call your local animal behaviorist and/or to watch The Dog Whisperer on t.v., while you and pooch are doing EFT For Animals together.

EFT For Our Animal Friends is exactly about helping our animal friends feel comfortable with themselves, and with us, so that they too can relax and enjoy life. This workbook is designed to help us aid the animals in our lives so that they can move beyond the danger, sorrow and harm that they have known. This workbook is also designed to help our animal friends achieve a life of inner stability and trust.

I remember that which brought me comfort when I was a child. Of course I think about the dogs and cats who lived with us, but more often I recall the peace that spending time with my horse gave to me. So much so that when things became overwhelming for me in life, I would fill my horse's manger with straw and curl up there, sharing with her the solitude and serenity of an afternoon nap.

Freedom:

Freedom is another important component of the human/animal relationship.

My greatest freedom when I was a girl, was riding with my horse alone, on a warm summer's day. We would meander down the dusty dirt roads to a wide creek that had a large hole in it. Large enough to provide a great swimming place for both of us. Leaving the saddle on the bank by the creek we would take a refreshing swim. My horse loved the cool water and enjoyed swimming with me floating above her back. All I had to do was to hold onto her mane or keep my arms around her neck. Cool and refreshed, we would dry off in the sun.

Later, we would saddle-up and start our assent up another dirt road that would take us far away from the noise of humanity. The land on these hills was, thankfully, owned by a large university nearby. The fields were reserved for farming and research of various varieties of grain, hay and corn. And so, horse and I would wander undisturbed for the afternoon. When the sun started to set, casting it's crimson and amber rays across the land, we knew it was time to return home.

Our animal friends not only bring us comfort and freedom, but they also love to play, often providing us with endless laughter and protection.

Play:

Whether you are walking, running, hiking, riding in the car, swimming or playing frisbee, your dog is right there, ready to play. They are up for any exercise and usually have far more endurance than most of us have. I know it's not saying much for me, but my little Westie who had legs approximately four inches long, could run circles around me.

And then there are the 'stick dogs' who beg us to "throw the ball, throw the ball, throw the stick"... endlessly. This statement conjures up a memory of Sweet Pea, laying supine on the sofa collapsed and exhausted from attempting to entertain Whinny. Whinny, a friend's Jack Russell Terrier, was visiting and had demanded that Sweet Pea throw a ball somewhere around the rate of one hundred throws an hour. Sweet Pea is done in and begging to end the ball toss and catch, but not Whinny.

Wondering how to revitalize Sweet Pea's flagging enthusiasm, Whinny would dip her tennis ball into her water dish and then jump onto Sweet Pea's chest, dripping water and saliva all over her. Fetch and catch dogs are ALWAYS ready to play throw, catch and throw again!!!! Always ready! Always!

Who doesn't enjoy the companionship of a loyal and playful dog when we go for a walk? Dogs are sympathetic, playful and sensitive to our needs. Comfort, companionship and peace...What could be better?

When winter comes it provides lots of deep soft snow which is always an invitation for man and beast to play. Dogs love snow and are the first to make tracks in it. Saint Bernards and other mountain dogs rescue and save lives in it, but the average dog just likes to play, roll in and chew the stuff.

Cats on the other hand take a different point of view. Cats prefer to lay in a safe, cozy window keeping warm while they watch the rest of us make fools of ourselves in the freezing cold snow. Once you have come to your senses and returned in from the snow and cold, kitty will come around, pleased to share a snack and a warm cuddle by the fire.

Horses don't mind the snow one bit. Our stable was designed so that the horses had access to an open paddock, enabling them to go in and out at will. They were out more than in, and could be seen standing out in the open, with snow flakes on their backs taking a snooze.

Once we had a large black and white pinto boarding with us. She was an amiable and agreeable older mare, who didn't mind when we hooked her bridle up with long lines, hopped onto our sleds and had her pull us up and down the snow covered roads. We found this trick useful once again while bringing a large pine tree that had been cut for Christmas back to the house.

Only once do I remember there being dire consequences while playing with animals. For a short time while we had a sweet nanny goat. Although she was thought to be my sister's goat, I had it in my head that it was too cold for nanny to be outside, so I brought her into the house. Mother returned home from work to find the goat frolicking on the sofa. Clearly Mother didn't think this was a good idea.

Goat was put outside, and sister and I were given an earful regarding nanny goat protocol. The worst of it was that when we returned from school the next day, Nanny was gone. I don't think either sister or I have forgiven our mother. I doubt that sister has forgiven me.

I never look back at the animals I have been fortunate enough to have shared life with and grade them according to who was 'the best'. They were all wonderful and each in his or her own way has left an imprint upon my heart. Those who made me laugh and those who protected me, are probably the pets I recall most often.

Laughter:

Our collie Laddie (such an original name) was an extremely intelligent dog. He didn't think that we were very smart, however, and every once in awhile he would try to get one over on us. During the 1950's and 1960's cat food in the can was truly a foul- smelling and revolting affair. While we didn't like it, Laddie thought that it was delectable. Remember that dogs clearly don't smell what humans smell. They routinely roll in the rotting remains of other animals, manure is a favorite, and it seemed that so was eating cat food.

Laddie knew that he was forbidden to eat the cat's food, but every once in a while he just couldn't help himself. After gulping down kitty's rations, he would make the fatal mistake of coming into the living room and betraying himself. My Father always called Laddie the politician, because he enjoyed shaking hands and could grin from ear to ear.

Feeling guilt over having eaten the cat food, he would come into the living room, grinning broadly and shake hands (paws) with anyone who happened to be there. Naturally, the stench of his cat food breath was a give away, and instead of garnering votes, he would be scolded for stealing the cat's food. You could feel sorry for the bewilderment in his deep brown eyes. I sometimes think he wasn't prone to self betrayal, but rather, I think he just couldn't understand how we knew.

One particular dog, a Boxer named Duchess would amuse herself by chasing a horse that was grazing in the pasture. Once the horse would get up to speed the tail would flow straight out behind it. Duchess would then grasp the long tail in her powerful jaws. One could be enjoying a quiet afternoon inside, and glance out the window to see Duchess being pulled through the air by a galloping horse. Of course this had to stop, so she was not allowed access to the pasture nor to galloping horses from then on.

Many years later I had a wonderful dog, a Bichon Frise named Poppy. She was a sweet, gentle, and loving creature. I just wished that she had kept her opinions to herself.

It so happens that I like to sing, although neither my children nor my animals appreciate my melodic expressions. Poppy didn't hesitate to share her opinions regarding my singing talent, or lack thereof, with me. When I would sing, she would cover her ears with her paws and whine. I accused Sweet Pea of teaching Poppy to do this. After laughing heartily at the dog's plaintive booing and my consternation, she disavowed all involvement.

Most of you have wonderful memories and stories to tell about the special animals who have shared life with you. Most of you would love to have a simple and effective tool that you can use to help them. EFT For Animals will enable you to do this. Please use this technique for your own animals, sharing your success and amazement with your friends. Our intention is to enable humans and animals to lead better, healthier and happier lives together.

Notes

CHAPTER TWO
HOW DOES EFT HELP ANIMALS?

We tend to forget that humans are animals too. We all spring from Mother Earth to create our individual existence, and we cannot live without her. Most Earthly life forms require clean oxygenated air to breathe. We derive nourishment from her fertile soil. We show up representing our type, our personality, our special color or genetic characteristics, forging our identities collectively and individually. We can be upright and bi-pedal, four-footed and furry, feathered, claw-footed, or scaley, but we all need food, shelter, water and love.

Anyone who has lived with, worked with or cared for animals knows that they are highly emotional beings. They love deeply and honestly. They love their young, their pack, pride, flock or family. I believe that one of the deepest and most painful wounds that a domestic animal can endure is the loss of its family, its mate and its offspring. Most of us are pack animals by nature and we feel frightened, vulnerable and terribly alone when we lose the safety and warmth of our family groups. Whether the young are taken from their herds, flocks, prides or families, terror imprints their emotional bodies from this moment on. This is why a puppy or kitten or a colt etc naturally cries for its mother when it is taken from her. An infant child would do the same.

Having no one else to bond with, they will out of need to survive, attempt to bond with the people in whose care they have found themselves, for better or for worse. Because they no longer live naturally in the wild, their ability to survive and provide for themselves has been lost. From then on, having become dependent upon others, they live in fear for their basic survival.

Therefore, one of the first things we want to tap our animal friends for is fear. Fear of being isolated. Fear of abandonment. Fear that they aren't or won't be cared for. Fear of being hurt. Fear of not being understood. Fear that they won't survive. Fear that they are not safe. Fear that there may not be enough to eat.

The second basic factor that we would tap for is the loss of home. Animals seek out and find safety in their dens, their nests, their caves or their houses. Most of the animals we have taken into our houses or shelters have lost their homes. Very few animals in this world are born, live and die in the same location. They are isolated, sold or given away to people and taken to places that are foreign to them. The new house smells foreign and not like home. The rules are different, and they are punished for breaking rules that they don't understand. They are saddened, traumatized and deeply confused. Even so, as adolescents, they exhibit a happy demeanor that is common to all of the Earth's children instinctually. They try to find happiness and playfulness regardless of difficult and challenging circumstances.

We will tap for:

- Fear of being homeless, past, present, or future.

- For not being safe in the home.

- For being confused and feeling unwelcome in the home.

- For not having a home or being lost in the streets.

- For being given away to someone else.

-   For having to share a home with others who reject or compete with them for position, food and attention.

-   And of course for specific injuries, illnesses and for negative behavior.

You may wonder why we are tapping on these basic issues rather than that kitty has a runny nose. Physical symptoms are more often than not linked to an emotional component. Maybe the suitcase has been taken out of the closet, and kitty knows that you are going away. It may be for a short vacation, but kitty doesn't understand that. Kitty feels familiar anxiety and basic fear of abandonment taking over. Kitty worries that she won't get the food or water she needs. Even if we could speak "kitty" and Kitty could speak our language, she would still be feeling anxious. Pain and doubt and a recurring sense of insecurity arise when she feels that she is being abandoned or is not safe. Simple reassuring words won't assuage kitty's fear, but key words accompanied by tapping will help.

Remember the first time you were dropped off at school or at camp? I bet you do. Panic, helplessness and despair, right? English-speaking human-child being left with others who speak English and try to comfort but desperation and fear take over.

Camp or school may have had a good and happy ending or it may not have, but the fear of abandonment, insecurity and loss remain logged in our memory banks. Our animal friends aren't one bit different from us in this regard. Unfortunately for them, however, they do not have their family members to come for them when camp is finished or the school day ends.

The beauty of EFT is that simple tapping seems to instantly disable the connecting emotional links which bind cause-and-effect together. I believe that there are many simple and uncomplicated natural biological systems that we have forgotten about in our development as a species. EFT offers us a way to discover and utilize a method of accessing and modifying patterns which make us seem stuck in a negative state. Try the following techniques with an open mind, and a heartfelt desire to help. Enjoy the confidence that this simple success will offer you and your animal friends.

Using EFT to help our animal friends, is probably one of the simplest and yet most rewarding things one can do to alleviate animal suffering.

CHAPTER THREE
WHAT ARE WE TAPPING FOR?

When we see an animal or a person who is suffering or in pain our natural instinct is to reach out with our hands to comfort. Our hands have innate healing ability, and I think that most of us are aware of this. When we have been injured or are in pain we always reach for the injured or painful area knowing that in some way this touch will alleviate the pain and hurt. When our children are in pain or troubled we instinctively reach for them, knowing that our touch will comfort and help them to feel safe. We reach for them also when we wish to feel loved and perhaps, in an emotional way, complete.

Animals aren't any different than we are. If a calf, a foal, a kitten or a puppy isn't well or has been injured, the mother or even some other sympathetic adult animal, will go to the one suffering to help quell its pain. They will also come to our aid whenever possible if we are stressed or in peril. This has been noted and confirmed over and over again. We have had movies dedicated to such animals. Television series such as Lassie and Rin Tin Tin impacted our hearts and delighted us with laughter.

Dogs are trained to serve and assist in battle. Many stray dogs have come to the aid of our soldiers in Iraq, giving each of them someone to love and to be loved by. Healing through the warmth and affection that touch provides transcends species.

The Bird Man Of Alcatraz has been immortalized because of the sensitive interaction he had with the birds he tended while in prison.

The soft roiling purr of a cat is comforting and soothing. This is why our words and voices are such an important factor in our healing work with animals. I suggest you read Messages From Water by Dr. Emoto.

Animals are now taken into hospitals and nursing facilities because it is a known fact that just their presence is a healing comfort for the patients.

My mother is living in a nursing facility, and every Friday the staff bring their animals to work. Their presence amuses and brings heart-warming energy to the patients. All of the animals add their own special characteristics to the blend of creatures, but the biggest hit is a pot bellied pig who is rolled around in a wheel chair. Of course, the sight of a piggie in a stroller makes everyone smile, but when he grunts a little the room fills up with peals of laughter. Touch heals and so does sound.

This is why we touch and use our words in Healing Our Animal Friends With EFT.

Why not just touch and speak kindly?

If you do touch and speak softly to your animals then you are already on the right track. The only thing missing is focused intention.

What does it mean to address our animals with focused intention? It means that we are focusing, gently, on eliminating a specific illness or behavior problem from the animal's database. Database? Which database are we talking about? We are referring to the information or data stored within each of us that affects us profoundly in every way.

The physical anatomy of most Earthly creatures, including homo sapiens, is very similar indeed. Except for invertebrates most have a brain and a spine complete with spinal fluid and nerve roots. Most of us have ribs and soft tissue to support and move us. Each type has a mouth, two eyes, two ears, a heart, intestines, a stomach, a liver and so on.

The brain and spine comprise command central. This is why we move slowly and delicately when we tap or stroke on the spinal area.

We are all similar in that we respond to life emotionally. From decades of experience doing this sort of healing it is apparent to me that this emotion is stored in the various cells within us. This is to say that emotion is physical. If we are going to heal negative emotion then we must address the physical self as well. This is why we tap or stroke the animals.

Emotional information is stored as memory located throughout our bodies. This information is derived from the basic imprints we come into life with, as well as from the data we acquire from our day to day experiences. This information is compiled and stored in the "appropriate" repository and can be retrieved again and again through stimulation. I don't want to get technical or medical with this, since I don't know the first thing about medicine or technology. So let's refer to this as the metaphorical database.

Which came first the computer or the egg?

Let's have some fun. Let's just see our anatomy and that of our animals as computers. Let's suppose that the sensory nerves of the animals we are helping comprise the Programer. This is the smart guy who tells the animal that this is what it smells, hears, touches and feels. This is what is going on outside of itself at the moment.

Let's suppose that the brain is the Monitor and the motor nerves serve as the Reactor or Responder, if you prefer. Therefore, hypothetically, the Programer senses something scary and wrong going on outside or inside of itself. It wants to warn the Monitor that there is danger. Before doing so it scans the database or files for anything previously stored that might factor in as similar to the incoming information. So, the "files" yield up stored memory of prior experiences which are similar in nature.

This information is bundled together with the new data and speedily transferred to the brain, now referred to as the Monitor.

The Monitor swiftly transfers this information to the Reactor, or motor nerves, which respond. Getting this information, our animal friend scoots, hides, crouches, flies away or hunkers down preparing for battle. This information is stored in our memory bank for further reference.

Does this system operate based only on negative emotion? No. But it is the negative that causes repetitive experiences to occur, as well as creating areas of stagnation and density within the body.

Where there is stagnation within the body, blood cannot circulate, lymph cannot move nor communicate properly and nerves cannot enervate adequately. Bad news.

Happy, loving, comforting experiences, at least in our metaphorical database, are expansive. These emotions carry love, light and health. This is the good news. So you can see that we heal in every way when the Programmer gives the body/mind continuum positive information.

Through this system of Healing Our Animal Friends With EFT we have a simple, easy way to reprogram the metaphorical database. We tap out the bad news. We tap in the good news.

Why can't we just tap in the good news? No two things in life can occupy the same space. Let's say, that we can blend and mix things together, but each maintains its own identity. In simple terms, one has to clean and empty out the closet before putting more inside. We also do not have to determine what to fill the newly opened and cleansed areas with. It's similar to scooping sand up at the beach. The water flows in.

Once we have sent the old, toxic, painful information to the recycling bin, the Light flows in leaving our pets lighter, brighter, happier, healthier and greatly relieved.

CHAPTER FOUR
FORMULA FOR TAPPING

Healing Our Animal Friends With EFT is a simple system of tapping or stroking gently along the body's energetic and physical pathways, with the intention of achieving improvement in the emotional and physical well-being of the animal we are trying to help. When we tap or stroke gently along the animal's spine we are encouraging the body's energetic pathways to open, discharging negative or imbalanced bio-energy. In the system being put forth in this book we are only interested in the energetic pathway that is located along the spine. You can tap successfully along the spine itself as well as the area which is close to the actual spine. There is no need to be exact. Again, our success with this technique has more to do with positive intention than point specificity.

Through this simple, easily understood method we can remove the emotional links that keep our animals bound to their limitations, frustrations, sickness, pain or other energetic disturbances. This principal applies to all the children of the Earth, whether they are human, canine, equine, bovine, serpentine or avian.

We are all as capable of healing as we are of suffering.

In the Introduction we mentioned that the EFT tapping points were designed for humans, and that they achieve the great results for which they were intended. In this workbook we are focused upon helping animals, therefore we tap along the spine.

This is not because animals don't have the same tapping points in their bodies as we do, nor that they would not respond favorably to the tapping. They might.

In this book we recommend using the spine for tapping with animals because most beings have a spine which is easily perceptible and accessible. If an animal is in distress or panicked it is apt to bite, claw or kick to defend itself. Tapping around the face, chest or feet of any creature that is in fear mode is pure foolishness.

Of course, it is best if you quietly and softly tap on the spine of the animal you are helping when they are resting or being groomed or even while asleep. If you are an animal professional then you may have to use humane methods of protection and restraint for the animals you are tapping.

Healing Our Animal Friends With EFT is not intended to replace veterinarian care or behavioral training for your pets. It is meant to assist and to enhance their care.

Helping your animals to prepare for and accept professional care is one of the benefits of this technique. Simple tapping or stroking on the spine gently and lovingly is a comfort to most animals. It helps them to trust and to relax. Our esteemed veterinarian was naturally skeptical of Healing Our Animal Friends With EFT because he hadn't yet tested it or seen the results for himself. He, of course, knew that my cat Luna was unusually calm and accepting of his examination, shots and the pedicure that she absolutely hates. But all of us should require evidence. In order to understand or to continue to use and appreciate anything, having evidence is a must. Recently I provided our veterinarian with the tapping technique and options so that he can use this in his practice and recommend this valuable method to others. While discussing Healing Our Animal Friends With EFT with him he did say that he was totally in favor of anything that would encourage people to spend caring time stroking and kindly handling their pets. Good for pet and person.

When do we tap?

As mentioned before, it is best to tap when you and your animal are at ease and not pressured or rushed. Preferably, when the household has settled down for the day, when the members of the household are out or minimally distracting.

All that is required is that your intention is to soothe and help. **Never make more than a few passes at a time.** This technique, which is simplicity itself, is very powerful. It won't benefit any of us to over-treat. In fact, it could be upsetting to the pet. Animals have emotions which are powerful. Most are highly sensitive and reactive. Over-tapping could be disturbing and overwhelming.

Releasing too much emotion or trauma at one tapping session is unbalancing and can frighten both animal and human alike. Be patient.

We have found that animals treated with EFT almost always go to their crates, beds or another safe and quiet place to sleep after their tapping sessions. Also, after experiencing the tapping a few times most animals come to us for more. I have had people share their stories with me. They tell me that their cat pats them with her paw when she wants to be tapped. Dogs often come and stare hoping you will get the message. Others like Ellie, whom you will read about later in this workbook, come and lie down by your feet. Ellie actually has a position that she enjoys for her tapping sessions. She lays on her belly and stretches out her front and back legs for her person, Jacky, to tap.

Now that we understand why we are using our hands, and we know how to use the hands for this technique. Let's discuss what issues we might be tapping for.

First, we determine the problem.

What alarming behavior is the animal exhibiting?

Is the animal in fear, grief, anger, sick or dreading being alone perhaps? If an illness is the issue use the specific illness as described by your veterinarian. We need to determine the nature of the problem.

Since we see how that animal reacts to various situations, we understand what the problem is, so that we can now work to eliminate the cause. Focus on one problem, or issue, at a time. Especially when this technique is new to you and to your animal.

Do not confuse the animal or yourself. Keep it simple. After you are accustomed to doing this you can combine issues, but not while learning. Now that you know what the issue is that you and your animal are working to resolve, the next step is to identify the emotional link to the problem.

Identifying the emotional link to the problem.

This is the critical step toward making this tapping session successful. Knowing which emotion the animal is feeling is easy. Just think what emotion this situation would generate within you. Or observe the animal for a while. Is it hiding or cowering? Then obviously it is experiencing fear and/or dread of something or someone.

If the animal is sleeping excessively, perhaps it is depressed and or sad. Sickness often arises from patterns of grief and depression. The loss of a friend, be it human or animal, can cause overwhelming depression in an animal, just as it would within us.

Is the animal aggressive or barking threateningly? Then clearly he is fearful but responding angrily. Using this information we now have the emotional links to the problem; fear and anger. This information is what we can use to disable the link to the problem.

Disable the link

We have determined the problem and the accompanying emotion. Let's say, "I am angry and frightened when the mailman leaves the mail, so I bark loudly and/or chew-up the mail." This sentence displays the problem and the emotional links to the problem. Now all that is left is to disable the emotional link to the problem. How do we do this? We use a phrase that nullifies the "charge" on the statement, such as "nevertheless I trust and accept myself completely". Affirming that the animal is comfortable and safe within itself will disable the link to the problem at hand.

A few more statements that will disable the emotional link to the

problem:

"I am sad when the family leaves me alone in the

house so I chew up Sally's slippers, or I pee where I shouldn't,

but I trust and love myself completely."

"I lunge at the dog next door because I'm afraid that he'll take my place at home, but nonetheless I trust and accept myself completely."

There are many examples of possible tapping options in the next chapter. I have devised a simple formula to help you remember the sequence of steps used in this technique.

Formula For Tapping

It is as simple as 1, 2, 3. Just remember the word "**DID**".

D - DETERMINE the problem for which you are tapping.

I - IDENTIFY the emotional link to the problem.

D - DISABLE the link.

1. **Determine the problem** - "I do not want to go to the vet"..

2. **Identify the emotional link** -"I am afraid that I will be hurt or left there"...

3. **Disable the link** - "but I trust and accept that I'll be safe."

D. I. D. A few possibilities:

Determine the problem: i.e. chewing things, aggression at home or on the "playground", unreasonable barking, trip to vet, boarder or groomer etc.

Identify the emotion that links the animal to the problem: i.e. fear, grief, frustration, insecurity, loneliness, sadness, anger etc.

Disable the link to the problem: i.e. by stating for instance "I

trust and accept myself completely" or "nevertheless, I love and

accept myself"

For Example:

1. **Determine the problem** - "I do not want to go to the vet"..

2. **Identify the emotional link** -"I am afraid that I will be hurt or left there"...

3. **Disable the link** - "but I trust and accept that I'll be safe." A typical example:

"I panic because I am afraid to go to the vet, but I trust and accept myself completely." Repeat your phrase two or three times while gently tapping or stroking down the spinal area. Tap and speak softly.

DO NOT OVER-TAP

It is not unusual for there to be a delayed reaction. It is not unusual for the animal to rest after a tapping session while the body reconfigures new information. It may take a day or two before the old energetic congestion is opened up and removed.

BE PATIENT

It is reasonable for the animal to take some time to adjust and to integrate the change into his new behavioral matrix. Use only a few very succinct words while tapping. Try to be consistent with those words with each pass. As mentioned previously we understand that with the exception of a few voice commands, animals do not speak our language. How do they understand our words? They do!!

I believe that animals have a higher sensibility than most of us. Perhaps they understand our unspoken intentions. Perhaps it is their extraordinary sensory and energetic perceptions that make it possible. We can only guess. However, when you see the quick and simple positive responses they have to this work you, like myself, will understand and just gratefully accept.

HOW DO WE KNOW WHEN TO STOP?

How do we know when the desired change has been achieved? The animal will stop exhibiting the negative trait that you have been tapping for. It may be a gradual lessening of the emotional tendency or illness, or the change may occur suddenly.

In any case, there will be a time when whatever you were focusing on has been remedied and the animal no longer exhibits the traits for which it was being treated.

Once the animal shows obvious signs of improvement it is time to consider what other "issues" you would like to help your friend with. Or perhaps it's time to help another of your animal friends.

Once an animal has been treated with this method it will always come to you for a little tapping and love. If all is well and you do not have a specific thing to focus on, just infuse the animal with words and taps that reinforce health, safety and happiness.

Now that some of the stored negativity has been removed from the database one can just stroke or tap in words that uplift its spirit and continue to add strength, balance and wellness to the body.

A few examples:

"I am healthy and my (problem) is gone. I know that I am well and safe"

"I am loved and cared for and all of my health problems are now gone."

"Now that I am well, I can live in health, balance, harmony and safety."

You get the idea. Enjoy.

Notes

CHAPTER FIVE
SOME D.I.D. TAPPING POSSIBLITIES

I would like to discuss in which direction to tap, head to tail or tail to head. I have a preference for tapping head to tail. If we touch an animal's head they can see us and sense our good intentions. When we come up from behind they may misread our intentions, or we may startle them. Either direction will work as well the other, but if you can, try tapping head to tail.

When is it best to tap? Unless it is an emergency situation, it is best to tap before the "event". Before taking your pet to the vet. Before the mailman arrives. Before the animal is left alone again etc.

It is possible to do this technique when the animal is in a higher state of excitement, but it is preferable to do this when they are more relaxed.

Please bear in mind that some animal traits such as clawing furniture, smelling less than sweet, rolling in unmentionable odious substances, normal barking and leaving fur all about the house are natural and instinctual and should not be considered to be "bad" behavior. We must accept the natural healthy behavior of our animal friends although it may be tiresome, inconvenient or unpleasant. It is a small sacrifice that we make for the pleasure they bring into our lives.

Let's review step by step:

STEP ONE: DETERMINE THE CAUSE OF THE PROBLEM Let's look at some possible tapping scenarios with regard to determining the cause of the problem.

- being kept in my crate (stall, cage,room or in the house) all day

- being taken to the vet or groomer

- going for a walk

- when children (people) scream

- when being hurt or threatened

- not liking or having enough food

- being left alone

STEP TWO: IDENTIFY THE EMOTIONAL LINK TO THE PROBLEM Using a few of the possible causes we mentioned previously as determinates, let's identify some possible emotional links.

Being left alone.

"I am angry and feel abandoned when I am left alone all day, so I"...

"I am depressed or nervous when I am left alone, so I"...

"When am left alone I feel anxious and trapped, so I"...

Going to the vet or groomer.

"I'm afraid of the vet, so I"....

"I am terrified that I will be hurt when going to the vet/groomer, so I"...

"I am afraid that I will be abandoned and left at the vet/groomer/boarding, so I"...

I fear not having control, so I"...

Walking:

"When I am walking on a leash, I am afraid I cannot get away from other animals, so I"...

"I pull on my leash/reins because I am nervous and want to run, so I"...

"I feel insecure and feel trapped when I am on a leash, so I"...

Noise:

Remember when animals hear yelling and screaming they believe that it is a warning and that there is danger. They can also believe that it is aggression and that they are in danger.

"I am afraid when I hear people yell or scream, so I"...

"When I hear someone cry I become fearful, so I"....

"When I hear a child cry I become concerned, so I"...

"Loud noise makes me think that there is violence, so I"...

Confinement:

"I hate/resent being trapped and kept in a cage (room, house stall etc), so I"...

"I am bored and sad to be kept in a stall or cage, so I"...

"I am depressed and nervous because I am trapped and cannot go outside, so I"...

"I am not getting enough exercise, so I"...

Handled harshly:

"It frightens/angers me to be handled harshly, so I"...

"I am hurt and fearful when my collar is pulled too tightly, so I"...

"I am in pain and distress when the bridle is yanked too tightly, so I"...

"I am stressed and frightened when I think I am going to be hit, or have my tail pulled, so I"...

Think about how you would feel in their situation, and you will understand the emotions which they are most likely feeling.

STEP THREE: DISABLE THE LINK

The following statements affirm a positive belief in oneself. This positive affirmation will balance, and therefore nullify, the negative behavior pattern.

"But I trust and accept myself completely."

"However I love and accept myself completely."

"Nevertheless I know I am fine and safe."

Use your words and ideas.

LET'S PUT STEPS ONE, TWO AND THREE TOGETHER.

Examples:

"I am angry and feel abandoned when I am left alone, so I chew up clothes or toys, but nevertheless I know I am safe and loved."

"I am depressed and/or nervous when left alone, so I pee on the floor. Nevertheless I trust and accept myself completely."

"When I am walking on a leash I lash out at other dogs because I am afraid and unable to get away if threatened. But I love myself and feel secure."

"I angrily pull on my leash because I am insecure and want to prove that I am a pack leader. But nevertheless I trust and accept myself completely."

"Leaving the house to go to the vet scares me. But I know that the vet will help me and my health will improve."

"Although I have been sick with....I know that I will heal and be well again. I know this because I trust and accept myself completely."

"I am so sad because (whomever) doesn't live here any more. But nonetheless I know that she/he will be fine. I know this because I trust and accept myself completely."

Notes

CHAPTER SIX
WHEN DOES EFT FOR ANIMALS NOT WORK?

This technique works swiftly. Do not attempt to speed-up or force the process.

Tap with healing kindness and patience.

Let your animal friend rest between tapping sessions. Wait a few days, or sometimes a week, and then tap again. It would not be surprising if the animal being treated comes to you for tapping sooner than you think. If this is the case, it would be okay to tap again.

Animals have a discerning instinct regarding what is best for them and what is not. If they indicate that they are ready to receive more tapping, then by all means, tap again. When they are allowed to be, animals are fairly self-regulating.

During the "resting" intervals, between tapping sessions, observe the changes the tapping has made. One cannot force the healing process, but we can create and allow it. Healing, of this nature, has a wisdom and an intellect of its own. Trust that and relax. Remember that you are the Programer. You decide what the problem is. You decide which emotional link you wish to disable. When you have used the tapping to disconnect the emotional link to the problem, new information is automatically sent to the Monitor. The Monitor(the brain) and the Responder (sensory nerve) know their duties, and will perform their functions, implementing new, positive behavior patterns.

The importance of finding the right emotional link

If you are not seeing a positive change in the animal being treated, then the first thing to look for is that you may not have used the emotion that the animal is feeling. Observe the animal and decide what other emotions it might be feeling. Try one and then another until you see long-lasting change. It may be having several strong emotions regarding the situation for which you are tapping. You can combine some of the emotions if you think it is appropriate.

For Example: "I am depressed and lonely since Sally went away to school, but I trust and accept myself completely."

Or perhaps: "I am frightened and feel abandoned now that Sally no longer lives here, but I trust/know that I am safe and loved."

Disabling the emotional link to the problem is the key to success. You are the Programer, and you decide which emotion or emotions are basic to the problem that you and your animal are solving.

If we do not include the causative emotion in the tapping statement, we will delay the success we are looking for. Keep using other emotions until you see a positive result.

You are probably wondering what difference our words make to the animal. As mentioned before, I understand that except for a few commands, animals do not speak our language. As amazing as it seems, the correct emotional words do make all the difference. How they understand, I do not know, but they do. You will see this for yourself as you practice your technique.

For Example:

If we say, while tapping lightly near the animal's spine,

"I bark when the mailman leaves the mail, but I trust and accept myself completely", this will not remedy the situation.

Where is the emotional link here?

We could say, "I am afraid when the mailman leaves the mail, so I bark to chase him away, but nevertheless I trust and accept myself completely."

We could say, "I am afraid and angry when the mailman comes to the house, so I bark loudly to make him go away. But I know that I am safe and loved."

The Programmer/Tapper must be someone whom the animal trusts and feels comfortable with

It is most important that the tapper be someone that the animal being tapped is comfortable with. Professionals, of course, do not have a personal relationship to an animal, but animals have an uncanny sense about who to trust and who not to. I believe they can smell our intentions.

Despite my words, my dog understands whether we are going out now or later. I may wave the leash and tell him that we are going out, but there are times when he just goes and lays down. He lives for his walks, but he can sense that a lot can go on between the declaration of a walk and the actual thing. He is always right.

The phone rings; delay. I spend too much time in the bathroom; another delay. I can't decide which boots to wear; delayed again. And so it goes. When my mind is actually made up, and I am ready to leave the house, he is waiting for me by the door.

You have had experiences with your pets which are similar, no doubt. Knowing that they clearly can sense accurately what is going on, you will agree that they instinctively know who is friend and who is foe. It is imperative that the person tapping be someone the animal feels at ease with. If the animal you are tapping has a particularly negative reaction to someone, it would be best for a more neutral person to do it. Needless to say, violent or impatient people should never handle the animal.

If you, or someone in the household, is violent or aggressive, then it would be a good thing to experience EFT yourselves before attempting it with your animals.

EFT would help you, your family members, or friends to relax and to be more at ease with yourselves, your lives and your animal friends. I do not recommend using the spinal method put forth in this book for humans. It is best to go to the EFT web site www.emofree.com to find a practitioner in your area. It would be a good thing to purchase the training videos which are available from the EFT web site.

These dvd's are affordable, and a valuable tool to have in order to help yourself, or your loved ones, find the peace and health they are seeking.

If a child or someone is tormenting the animal then they must stop. You cannot convince a pet that someone who screams or throws things can in any way be trustworthy. We suggest that if you know such a person, that you tap that person regarding their aggressive tendencies, until others can feel safe in their presence.

CONSIDER THE OPTIONS

If you are feeling that this technique is not working as you would like, take some time to ponder the situation, so that you can identify the key emotion.

For instance, is it that the cat just doesn't like humans and stays aloof, or is it, perhaps, that the "other" cat is the dominant one, and threatens the aloof cat, claiming sofa and lap as its own?

Look into each situation. Ask yourself questions about what might really be going on. Ask family members for their perspectives.

Listen to their points of view. We all see things a little differently, and it might be that slight difference that gives us the key to the solution

Remember to always speak softly, use a light touch, and make only a few passes during each tapping session.

Tapping too hard

Sometimes when an animal refuses to be tapped it is because the touch is too hard. If you soften your touch they will usually relax and willingly submit to your touch. Just barely touch the surface of their bodies, or gently brush your hands back and forth across the spinal area, head -to -toe a few times. Let your touch be a healing tool. The warmth of a kind and well-intentioned hand will comfort and assure the animal of your goodwill.

Session too long

When animals have reached their limit, they will leave or draw away. When they get the idea that this is helping them, they will come to you for tapping of their own accord. Allow them to find their own tolerance and limits to the sessions. There will be animals who totally love this and cannot get enough. Others may be a little skeptical. Be tolerant and loving, giving them all the respect and patience that you can.

If you have cats, then you already know that they understand what a necessary gift kneading and tapping can be. My cat puts me to sleep at night, and wakes me up in the morning, by doing her little tap dance on my back, chest or head.

Too much noise or distraction

Try to find a quiet time, when you and the animal you are tapping, can be relaxed and undisturbed. You will progress faster and get a better result if you select your tapping times and locations carefully, keeping privacy and quiet in mind.

Not certain what the problem actually is

Ponder the animal and its reactions to things. Ask friends, family and the "inner-self" for their input. Especially ask young children what they think is wrong with "fifi", "fido" or "trigger". They have a clarity of mind that is all their own. They are often unencumbered with logic and less clouded by ego. They may also have spent more focused time alone with their animals, having time to tune-in and feel the pulse of the animal, so to speak.

Too little patience

Select a time to tap the animals when you are relaxing or at rest. If you don't take time to relax or rest, perhaps a good time for the tapping might be before bedtime. Perhaps on the weekends, when you get up more leisurely, and the day doesn't begin with an alarm clock.

Relax and have fun with this. Do a little yoga. Perhaps take a hot bath. Relax and tap for fun and for the well being of your animal friends.

CHAPTER SEVEN
ADDRESSING IMBALANCED BEHAVIORAL PROBLEMS

At times our animals behave in ways that we just don't understand. Their behavior indicates that they are anxious, frightened or depressed. They might exhibit unhealthy behavior in many ways. We have indicated some of those aberrant behavior patterns that are rather common. Just use your best guess and tap while declaring that, although the animal has this problem they..."trust and accept themselves completely". Do not worry that you may not be exactly accurate at first. Change the emotional links and look more deeply into the possible reasons for the problem. Eventually, if you think about it and persist, you will have the positive change that you are seeking.

Last summer while visiting my 97-year-old aunt, I taught her to do EFT on herself. She taps every day and tells me that she can alleviate the pain she has in her arthritic knees, and can therefore sleep soundly at night. She tells me that although she still has a blockage in her intestines the doctor, clearly bewildered, told her that the blockage is getting smaller. She is now going to take on her fading eyesight, and I have no doubt, will succeed in creating an improvement. When she tells me what she is saying, and where she is tapping, I smile and tell her that she is doing great. Obviously she is. She does not reiterate the prescribed phrases I suggested, but makes up her own as she goes along. She does not tap on the hand where I showed her to tap but on other areas of her hand. The point I am trying to make here is that this is not a rigid or exact science.

Trust your hunches and instincts, tap lightly on the animal's back a few times, and you will create the result you are hoping for, a healthy, happy animal friend and, therefore, a happier you.

Some possible tapping options

Excessive Barking or Whining

"I bark because I am hurt that no one listens to me, but I trust and accept myself completely."

"I bark or whine because I am lonely and feel left out, but I know that I am loved and safe."

"I bark because I am afraid to be left alone: I miss my pack, but I love and accept myself completely."

Digging up the yard or the carpet

"I am anxious when I don't get enough exercise, so I dig to burn off my frustration, but nevertheless I trust and accept myself completely."

"I get angry and frustrated when I don't get enough attention or love, but nevertheless I love and accept myself completely."

"I am nervous and bored so I dig to burn off excess energy, but nevertheless I trust and accept myself completely/'

"I am angry and dig up the yard/carpeting when (fill in the blank), but I trust and accept that I am safe and protected."

Stealing Food or Tearing up Items

This might be a dog that doesn't know its place within the pack. Training for your dog and yourself with a skillful animal trainer would be helpful.

"I resent that I don't get the food I need/want, but I trust and accept myself completely."

"I resent that you leave me all day, but I trust and accept myself completely."

"I am frustrated because my food doesn't satisfy me, but I trust and accept that I am healthy and cared for."

"I am afraid that (what's its name) will eat all the food and I will have none, but I trust and accept myself completely."

Pet leaving its 'mark' of the floors or furniture

"I am nervous when I don't get enough kindness and attention, so I dig and chew, but nonetheless I trust and accept myself completely."

"I am insecure and need to know that this is my safe home, but I trust and accept that I am loved and safe."

"I hate being left alone, so I leave my mark for protection, but nevertheless I trust and accept myself completely."

"I am frightened of someone or another animal in the house or even next door, but I trust and accept myself completely."

When animals are old and/or sick

"I'm sad and embarrassed when I cannot protect myself and others, but I trust and accept that all is well."

"I feel lonely and frustrated when I am ignored, but I trust and accept myself completely."

"I feel that I am no longer loved and appreciated now that I am old and/or sick, but I trust and accept that all is well."

"I feel sick and/or in pain, but I trust that I can be well and pain free."

Adding a new member to the household

"I resent that I have to share attention and affection with..., but nevertheless I trust and accept myself completely."

"I feel sad and left out now that this new person/animal has come into our lives, but I trust and accept that all will be well."

Being a new member of a household, stable, flock etc.

"Being new to this family makes me scared and I feel threatened, but I trust accept myself completely."

"Being new to this herd is dangerous and scary for me, but I know that I can find a safe place within it."

"I feel isolated and scared because I am new to this household and family, but I trust and accept that all will be well."

"I feel isolated, alone and confused in this new home, but I trust and accept myself completely."

"I feel vulnerable and unsafe in this new environment, but I trust and accept myself completely."

"I'm afraid and sad and miss my old life and home, but I know that I will be loved and well-cared-for."

Notes

CHAPTER EIGHT
INSPIRATION

Jacky and Ellie.

With their permission, I am using Jacky and her dog, a five year old boxer named Ellie, as a way to illustrate why we will benefit only by being sensitive and patient with our animals.

Jacky rescued Ellie from another family who often kept her locked in the basement. We only know what we are told when adopting a pet; it's sort of like buying a used car. Jacky, her husband and their three young children realized soon after bringing Ellie home that she exhibited aggressive behavior, especially around food and other dogs. Ellie didn't hesitate to bite, and she immediately assumed an alpha dog position in the household. Jacky and her husband then started watching the Dog Whisperer on television. They learned a great deal and began implementing what they had learned.

Ellie's behavior improved, but she was clearly not domesticated enough to be alone with the children. If children went too near her food bowl, played too loudly, or if other children played in the house too, would Ellie's instincts create a defense mechanism that could result in violent behavior?

Jacky has had personal experience with EFT and I suggested to her that she try doing it with Ellie. I gave her the phrases and focus that I found helpful with other animals. These particular phrases had helped other friends and their pets with amazingly quick and easy results.

Jacky started tapping and using words that described emotions she knew Ellie was feeling and reacting to. After her "sessions", Ellie would retreat to her crate where she felt safe and undisturbed and would fall asleep. An interesting note is that whenever Jacky would tap around Ellie's loss of mother and litter mates Ellie would immediately get up and walk away. Separation anxiety is basic and common to nearly all domesticated animals. The trauma of being taken away from the safe comfort of the litter and nurturing of the mother is logged deeply and indelibly into the subconscious database. It is because of the depth of this pain that we work gently, slowly and patiently. Whenever Jacky tapped Ellie she left this painful memory of loss and fear for last. Ellie only tolerated one pass with the message before retreating to her crate. This continued for a few weeks until one day Ellie sat through three passes around her loss of litter and mother. Jacky followed up with a pass confirming Ellie's acceptance of her new "litter mates" - the children in the house.

It wasn't long before Ellie walked calmly by Jacky's side. She stopped fearing or reacting negatively to other dogs. She began to display traits of submission and trust by letting Jacky sit beside her on the floor to rub her belly.

She began to accept the children near her food and sat patiently while her dish was filled. Slowly Ellie stopped reliving the terror, loneliness and the pain that resided within her because of this primal loss. She felt safe in her new "pack". Like the ugly duckling she may have had an uncomfortable beginning, but she has matured into a family member. She feels at home.

Pictures of Jacky and Ellie

LUNA

Luna, my cherished companion, is an absolutely gorgeous calico cat. Recently Luna was diagnosed with kidney disease. After a lengthy conversation with Luna's veterinarian I learned that kidney disease in cats is usually not reversible; the bad news. However if the kidneys are rehydrated as the disease progresses then she would not be in terrible discomfort; the better news.

Although this news was a slight relief to me it couldn't eradicate the sadness I felt. I would not want to see any animal suffer, and the thought that I might be losing my dear friend was very painful and disturbing. Painful, disturbing and unacceptable.

What to do?

EFT For Our Animal Friends, of course.

Her vet recommended that she be put on low-protein cat food.

I offered her both the wet and dry food that was recommended by her Vet. She would eat the dry food reluctantly but was absolutely not having the wet food. So I continued feeding her the wet food that she was accustomed to.

When we began the above routine, Luna had lost about one pound of her usual healthy weight. Her fur was oily and appeared a little stringy. She wasn't communicating a lot and would sleep considerably more than usual. She knew that she was not feeling like herself and would cling to me for comfort and warmth.

Once the tapping started she would look forward to it and ask for this often. She loves it. Gradually she started perking up.

Her eyes became less dull and worried. Her pelt started to look healthy. It was beginning to look full and lustrous again.

She became more sociable. As time went on she began "talking" quite a bit. This was new. In the past she never had much to say. When she did "speak" her meow was weak and sounded like an old lady's squeak. Now she sounds definite and very sure of herself and the expression of her feelings. This makes me smile. It's so unlike her, and yet so delightful to have her interacting in this way. We continued the healing protocol, making sure that I tapped her at least once daily but generally two or three times a day. I would tell her that, although she had a temporary problem with her kidneys, she would recover and live a long and healthy life. Frequently I changed the words that I used, going with whatever seemed most accurate and appropriate at the moment.

The tapping was always light and slow, drifting down her spine gently using phrases such as...

"I'm afraid that my kidneys have been stressed and are struggling, but I know that I can heal and will be in perfect health again."

"I worry because my body chemistry is imbalanced and my kidney stressed, but I have no doubt that I can recover fully, living in health and long lasting wellness."

"Although I am weary and worried that my kidneys are not functioning perfectly, I know that I will heal and be well."

Three months later Dr. C., her veterinarian, retested her blood and urine. Then the call came from his office. As I expected and hoped, they told us that she would be fine.

Happy Day!!

Never doubt that tapping with EFT For Our Animal Friends will help. It will not prevent death from eventually calling us or our animals to that great green pasture, doggie park or open blue sky in heaven but it can always help out animals to live better, healthier and happier lives.

Try it. Be conscientious, consistent, persisent and trust. It will work for you.

The previous information regarding the easy successes we have had with Ellie and with Luna are meant to inspire you. It's a way to let you know that you can do EFT For Our Animal Friends just as easily as we have done.

Please share with us your success stories. Check our web site and blog to gain further knowledge and inspiration from others who have subscribed to this form of healing for animals. We will all learn from and teach each other as we go along.

Chance at the Beach

Happy tails.

Happy Tapping

AUTHOR

Andrea V. Christos has been a natural healing therapist for nearly forty years, employing a variety of healing and restorative modalitics in her practice. EFT has become a preferred option because it is a simple and effective tool that she can share with her clients so that they may use this technique to help themselves, their families, friends and the animals that they care for.

She believes that we all wish to live healthier, happier and more meaningful lives but often lack the tools to make the changes we desire and deserve. EFT is a remarkable technique that anyone can master for redesigning and creating a healthy, balanced and personally empowered way of living for humans and animals alike.

After using EFT with several animals it was clear to her that this was a healing tool that could also be used to relieve animal suffering. The sheer simplicity of this technique and the astonishingly swift response that animals have to it make it a useful tool for anyone to help their animals live harmonious, well-adjusted lives, free from the trauma of emotional and physical suffering that is unfortunately common to domesticated animals of all kinds.

Andrea is convinced that after you try EFT For Our Animal Friends a few times you too will discover the joy of helping those you care for to be healthy and content. Share your newly found successes with your friends and with us at www.eftwithanimals.com.

PROCEEDS

Twenty percent of the proceeds of this book are donated to Non-Profit Animal Rescue Agencies, and used to establish a training program for those who wish to learn and teach EFT For Our Animal Friends.

MEMORANDUM

A place to date and make notations. Chart your progress as you go. Record your finds: ideas and suggestions. Share with us and with others.